THE
BUMPER
BOOK
OF
LIES

BY
ATTILA THE HUN
(TRANSLATED FROM THE LATIN BY
SHAUN HUTSON)

Crombie Jardine
PUBLISHING LIMITED

13 Nonsuch Walk, Cheam, Surrey, SM2 7LG
www.crombiejardine.com

Published by Crombie Jardine Publishing Limited
First edition, 2005

ISBN 1-905102-37-2

Cartoons by Bob Gibbs
Designed by www.glensaville.com
Printed & bound in the United Kingdom by
William Clowes Ltd, Beccles, Suffolk

HOW TO USE
THIS BOOK

Congratulations. You are now the proud
owner of THE BUMPER BOOK OF LIES.
Perhaps you bought it for yourself or
maybe it was a present. You may even have
stolen it. Whatever the case, it is now yours
until your death, until you are mugged
and it is ripped from your dying fingers or
until you get bored with it and decide to
throw it away or give it to someone else.

If you do decide to throw it away then
please remember that it is completely
biodegradable and will not in any
way, shape or form create any more
huge holes in the ozone layer.

If you want to find an entry on a particular
subject simply go to the index. Every entry
is in alphabetical order. After that, you can

go to the contents page. Then you can go
to the pub. Or the cinema. Or the zoo.

This book was printed on re-cycled paper.
Re-cycled mainly from trees that have
been hacked down in the rain forest.

There is a special limited edition
completely inked in human blood and
scrawled on pages of dried human flesh.
This is available by mail order, direct from
the publishers or from Cell 18, Rampton.

If you wish to read about King Darius
of Persia then you are out of luck, sorry.
However, the word Persia appears at
least twice and the word King makes an
appearance upwards of forty times.

Elsewhere you will find everything
you always needed to know about
anything at all. Every single entry is
cross-referenced with other books and
there is an exhaustive bibliography
at the back of the book just after

the author's list of convictions.

A children's edition is also available with full colour illustrations and diagrams and a wipe clean cover.

As you will notice, the entry concerning PORNOGRAPHY is also printed on wipe-clean pages.

If you can't find what you are looking for in the book itself then please try the website www.porkies.co.org.uk. If you're still stuck, then telephone the author or the publishers direct on: (44) 020 8999 9999 and someone will be pleased to tell you where you can find adult education classes in your area.

So, enter a world of lies right now and, remember, absolutely everything you read is true.

ARCHITECTURE

THE STUDY OF SHARP INSTRUMENTS.

One of the most famous examples of
ARCHITECTURE is the CENOTAPH in
LONDON. Designed by SIR FRANCIS
DRAKE in 1912 to commemorate the
discovery of POTATOES, it stands
in OXFORD STREET where it was
originally supposed to serve as a traffic
sign. It was transported to Whitehall in
1920 and has since been the site of the

Annual Remembrance Day Service. The original design showed a British soldier bayoneting a surrendering German but this was thought too radical an anti-war comment, as was the inscription "UP YOURS, FRITZ", and QUEEN VICTORIA requested that the design be altered.

Architects train for anything up to a week before being allowed to design their first building. THE LOUVRE in PARIS was originally intended to be a small boulangerie and coffee shop but the initial plans were passed by GHENGIS KHAN on the advice of his second wife, PRINCESS GRACE OF MONACO, and the final edifice proved to be larger than was originally intended.

PARIS [*1] is home to many famous architectural wonders including:

- NOTRE DAME (designed by VICTOR HUGO) and constructed

[*1 see COLLABORATORS]

entirely of balsa wood.

- The SACRE COEUR, a small recording studio on the banks of the Seine, designed by MARCO POLO.

- The EIFFEL TOWER, built by EDITH PIAF to mark the liberation of Paris by the German Army in 1940.

- And, of course, the famous ARC DE TRIOMPHE, the huge triangular glass structure which houses one of NAPOLEON'S testicles and is inscribed with the name of every single person who ever bought a CHARLES AZNAVOUR album.

∏

∏ATURAL
HİSTORY

The study of all living and inanimate life forms on earth including the boring ones like plants which, on the whole, do very little worth writing about (except the carnivorous ones such as the SOUTH AMERICAN MERCENARY TULIP).

The earth is populated by more than thirty-seven different species of living creature. Some scientists have attempted to make the case for the existence of billions of species of animals and birds. This has

been disproved as a myth perpetuated by scientists who went to University and think they are above everyone else.

CHARLES DARWIN, after sailing single-handed around the world in his ship TITANIC, wrote in his classic work, 'ON THE ROAD', that there were probably close to fifty different kinds of rocks on the planet. But Darwin was a notorious alcoholic and his theories were dismissed by other naturalists of the time.

Darwin is celebrated for having discovered the GALAPAGOS ISLANDS, a volcanic outcrop of rocks just south of Guadeloupe, famous for types of animals not seen in other parts of the world. Particularly notable among the denizens of this large island is the GIANT TORTOISE. Darwin hypothesised that this creature was the forerunner of the modern GREYHOUND, mainly due to its incredible speed over short distances. Tests showed that this

gargantuan reptile could reach speeds in excess of eighty miles an hour, far faster than the so-called 'fastest animal on earth', the SIBERIAN TREE BADGER. Also present on the Galapagos and noted by Darwin, was the BLUE NOSED GANNET, an enormous flightless bird that lives exclusively in the nests of ARMY ANTS and feeds on its own young – two of the reasons that it was dangerously close to extinction even when Darwin first encountered it.

A close relative of the DODO, the GANNET was a tame and trusting creature with no visible inclination to defend itself. It was slaughtered in its millions by RUSSIAN PIRATES [*1] who landed on the Galapagos in the fourteenth century in search of string. Unable or unwilling to fly away, the gannets were wiped out by the pirates who used their leathery beaks to make knitting needles.

[*1 see VODKA]

Most animals live in AFRICA, a country discovered by DOCTOR LIVINGSTONE, his friend STANLEY and the singer/songwriter MUNGO JERRY. Africa boasts more than five species of animal, some of which roam the icy tundra of that country in large groups or GAGGLES.

The most easily recognisable is, of course, the LION. The lion is a solitary animal that lives in burrows close to riverbanks and exists on a diet of bread, petit fours and rice.

The most vicious predator of the area is the WEAVER BIRD. This enormous carnivore captures its prey using a BOLAS made from strands of vine that it meticulously sews together. It flies over the tundra then swoops down on its prey, ensnaring it in the huge net it carries. When the net is in place, the weaver bird uses the bolas to garrotte its prey. It then flies back to its nest to devour its victims at is leisure. Often

with other members of its family or HIVE.
It then decorates the outside of its nest
with the bones. One of the African tribes
that farm the tundra has an elaborate
coming of age ritual involving the weaver
bird. The young men [*1] of the tribe are
prodded with sticks by tourists until they
become so enraged they rush off to one of
the nests and attempt to steal a throw rug
or a small piece of bedside furniture from
the weaver bird. Once the furious bird
gives chase, the young man must do battle
with it armed only with a can opener and
a short spear called a BAZOOKA. Battles
of this kind can take anything up to three
days and usually end with the young
man being fatally wounded or, indeed,
proving his manhood by safely returning
to his village with an occasional table.

[*1 see MICHAEL JACKSON]

❖ 14 ❖

I

İnsECTS

There are over twenty species of insect in NORTH AMERICA alone. It has been estimated that, should there ever be a NUCLEAR WAR [*1], the only creatures to survive will be insects. This seems highly unlikely as many wasps cannot even survive a clout from a rolled-up newspaper, but insects are remarkably resilient.

Several insects are dangerous to man, not least of which is the MOTH. This unpredictable and vicious insect lays a clutch of two eggs in the wardrobe of its host and when the eggs hatch the

[*1 see GEORGE BUSH]

young impersonate the householders
by dressing in their clothes and
throwing elaborate dinner parties.

RUSSIA alone has more than five species
of WATER-BOATMAN. These insects
are so called because their heads are
shaped like oars and they frequently grow
beards. On clear summer evenings they
can often be heard singing, 'What shall
we do with the drunken sailor?' The
Chernobyl water-boatman is roughly the
size of a destroyer and feeds on spinach
that grows in small baskets around the
marshy land that the insects inhabit.

GREAT BRITAIN is best known for its
BEES. Playful creatures the size of tennis
balls, they are easily recognisable by their
colouring of green and white stripes. Bees
are aquatic and are often kept as pets.

The sworn enemy of the bee is the
LADYBIRD, a microscopic insect hated by

farmers because of its habit of hijacking combine harvesters and crashing them wantonly through fields of potatoes. The IRISH POTATO FAMINE of 1136 has been blamed on two or three ladybirds (known by naturalists as ROGUES).

Most interesting of all insects is the ANT. Thought by many scientists to be the ancestor of man, these multi-coloured creatures live in colonies of nine or ten and are highly intelligent. At least two ants have won the NOBEL PRIZE FOR LITERATURE and another received an Oscar nomination for best supporting actor in the classic film 'CAN YOU KEEP IT UP DOWNSTAIRS?' [*1]. An ant goes through several stages of growth, beginning as an egg before transforming into a rock then progressing into a sponge before reaching full maturity at the age of thirty-seven when it usually marries and has a family, undergoing a small

[*1 see GENITALS]

financial crisis when it approaches forty.

Darwin observed that ants were perfectly capable of piloting aircraft as well as being one of the few creatures on the planet capable of successfully creating a soufflé.

WAR POETRY

Very popular during the reign of
VLAD DRACULA in 24 B.C., poetry
has flourished during almost every
war in history. It became so popular
during the FIRST WORLD WAR that
a special unit of troops was raised
to fulfil the need for songs and odes
composed while under mortar fire.

The Queen's Own ARGYLE AND
SUTHERLAND FUSILIER POETS fought
with great bravery at the THIRTY-
SECOND BATTLE OF MONS in 1923
but were slaughtered. Many military

experts believe this is because they were armed with pens instead of rifles. Best known of the war poets was VIDAL SASSOON who was concussed, gassed, shot and cooked on a low heat for fifteen minutes at the battle of TRESEMME. He penned the immortal classic 'THE GAS' from which these poignant lines were taken:

The gas it gasses.
Oh I hate the gas and its gaseous gassiness.
That I should be gassed is ghastly.
Gas is everywhere.
Gas gasses all those who would remain
un-gassed and yet are still gassed by gas.
How will we stop the gas?

He went on to compose another classic, 'BULLETS', a portion of which is as follows:

Oh the bullets.
Bullets all around.
Bullets fired from guns.
Bullets that blow pieces of my friends off.
Bullets. Bullets.
God I hate bullets.

Sassoon surrendered twice but returned to his unit and went on to open a very successful garden centre after the war. He went insane and committed suicide by beating himself to death with a garden gnome but not before he'd written these other classic pieces:

'IS THAT TOMMY ON THE BARBED WIRE?'
'BLOODY GERMANS!'
'RAT STEW AGAIN?'
'A FOOTBALL MATCH IN NO-MAN'S LAND? ARE YOU FUCKING SHELL-SHOCKED?'

F

FİSH

"As man inhabits the earth, so do fish inhabit the sky in all their myriad numbers and with wings and stuff like that." So said SHAKESPEARE in his famous EUROVISION SONG CONTEST entry 'ODE TO A BUSH'.

The scientist MOZART once estimated that there were more than seventeen species of fish in the world. Some live on the land but usually only for minutes at a time. Most prefer small plastic bags at fairgrounds or glass tanks which people keep near their microwave ovens in their houses.

The most common species of fish is the COD, a large, carnivorous creature famous for its short temper and liking for Burberry patterned hats. The cod was responsible for the infamous Cod War of 1812 which saw huge armies of fish swimming backwards and forwards in the Thames and several other rivers shouting insults at each other and making obscene gestures with their fins.

Fish were discovered by the naturalist C.A.P. BIRDSEYE who maintained that they inhabited small cocoons made from breadcrumbs and lived in boxes. This idea was later disproved by Doctor Edward FINDUS, a jewel thief and part-time cardiographer, who postulated that fish were actually genetically related to man. This assumption being based on the fact that some human beings can be taught to swim and that some fish can be taught to play the mandolin.

Findus also discovered, with the help of his colleague DOCTOR JOHN WEST, that the SHARK was not actually a fish but a small town just outside BERLIN.

WHALES are often thought to be fish but are in fact amphibians related to NEWTS. Unfortunately, this case of mistaken identity did not prevent them being hunted practically to extinction by fleets of ships that chased them for their fur and the thick, fatty substance that they keep under their skin called CHEESE.

HERMAN MELVILLE, the journalist, wrote a very famous book about a huge whale. Published in 1943, 'HOW GREEN WAS MY VALLEY' is a terrifying story of a man, a fishing rod and a very large pond.

The KILLER WHALE is a particularly nasty specimen which preys upon dogs and other food it finds floating on the icebergs of the South Pacific. It disguises itself

as driftwood then leaps on its prey and
batters them to death with a large anvil.

Less well known is the FLAT WHALE.
Sometimes growing up to four miles
in width, these placid but useless
animals are often mistaken for islands
and settled. The Isle of Sheppey is in
fact an overgrown flat whale. As is
MANHATTAN, the capital of America.

Fish feed mainly on sand. Some fish feed
on other fish and are easily distinguishable
from their vegetarian cousins by their
markings. For instance the TIGER
FISH is very similar in appearance to
a milk carton, while scientists have
never actually properly identified the
incredibly savage KODIAK BEAR FISH
as anyone who has ever encountered
it has been horribly maimed, killed
and eaten. Or so scientists believe.

Living in the most remote and deepest

parts of the sea is the DEEP FISH. Shaped like a submarine, it was used by both sides in the Second World War to eat merchant ships. The Deep Fish can live for anything up to two hundred years and, once domesticated, will feed quite happily on everything from breakfast cereal to Jehovah Witnesses.

People often keep fish as pets. Left in a small hutch in the garden, fish will live for up to five minutes unless equipped with an aqua-lung.

T

TREES

Very large, very old and very boring, like politicians, these kings of the flower world can live for thousands of years if they're not chopped down and turned into cars. Trees are dependent on many different environmental conditions to help them thrive.

Of the nine million and five species that cover up to nine-tenths of the planet's surface, most trees are of the genus MDF. These magnificent specimens flower up to forty times a year and have branches shaped like sofas.

The FIR tree is often found in packs roaming the plains of New Guinea where it feeds on pebbles.

The WEEPING WILLOW is in fact falsely named, as it is a very happy tree that enjoys KARAOKE and BINGO but does have a tendency to suffer from baldness.

Most rare of all trees is the OAK. There are probably less than three of these massive trees in the world today, mainly due to the mindless actions of pygmies who chop them down and use them as stilts.

A great deal has been written about the future of the RAIN FOREST. This is a very small expanse of trees inside the foyer of the Holiday Inn, Basildon. As a great deal has already been written about the Rain Forest, it is not my intention to go over the same tired old ground again. The entire problem has been overstated anyway and numerous famous scientists

have gone on record as stating that the
world would probably be better off without
the Rain Forest anyway as it is home
to lots of nasty animals that can make
even the bravest men soil themselves.

The BANGKOK LARCH, which grows
on the slopes of MOUNT ETNA in the
HEBRIDES, is a particularly interesting tree
as it moves from place to place to improve
its chances of survival. These magnificent
trees offer shelter to political prisoners
and are also used in salads. The way to
tell the age of a tree is simply to ask it.
However, should the question be phrased
wrongly then there is the strong possibility
of injury as trees are very sensitive about
their age and even more sensitive about
their inability to speak. Approach the tree
downwind with a large axe or chainsaw,
distract it by throwing pieces of bread then
hack it down quickly and count the rings
on the inside of the trunk. This won't tell

you the age of the tree but it will prevent the possibility of the tree attacking first.

The GIANT CANADIAN REDWOOD can grow to heights of over eighteen thousand feet and is often used in the Mexican art of BONSAI. This is a popular hobby, invented by the Revolutionary PANCHO VILLA during the Russian Revolution of 1962 and involves eating bark (the hard knobbly matter that covers the roots of all trees except the BARKLESS TREE OF TIBET).

Many Japanese KAMIKAZE pilots carried trees into battle during the First World War as good luck charms.

The life cycle of a tree is incredibly complicated and many scientists over the years have gone insane trying to figure out how what begins as an egg can transform itself into a collection of twigs and leaves by the time it is less than two years old.

 The answer is CROSS-POLLINATION. This is a term used by people on science programmes to explain the reproductive cycle of the tree. Briefly, a male tree performs an elaborate dance to attract the attention of the female. It then inserts its massive trunk into the female whereupon it is caught in the female's web and devoured. Other members of the natural world, including the GECKO, a small piece of sponge that inhabits caves in Estonia, have copied this process.

A tree was the first living creature to complete a circuit of the earth in a rocket.

T

TRANSPORT

When the first man (ERECTUS ENGINEERUS) invented the car back in the Jurassic Period, little could he have realised how invaluable transport was to become. Unfortunately, the wheel wasn't discovered until over two million years later during the RADIAL epoch so cars in early times had to be pushed everywhere.

The FORD STEGOSAURUS was the first mass-marketed vehicle and had one engine in the front and another in the back. It fed on bushes.

EGYPT saw transport come into its own with the invention of the CHARIOT. This heavy, armour plated vehicle was used to build the PYRAMIDS which were used as garages. Around the same time, the TRAIN began to be taken more seriously and tracks were laid between Cairo and Luxor for the train to run on. These were made of reeds and were frequently eaten by locusts, necessitating the need for replacement on a daily basis.

The Egyptian Czar, NECROPOLIS III, ordered the ISRAELITES to build more train tracks and this is what caused the famous TWELVE PLAGUES OF EGYPT, spoken of in the BIBLE. Trainspotting in Egypt became practically impossible after these plagues, especially as the last, and most potent, was the death of the First Born Driver. When the Angel of Death descended on Egypt it killed all those living in houses that hadn't

been smeared with camel droppings. These droppings were used to power the trains, and as the drivers were usually very forgetful thousands died when the curse arrived on the 3:10 from Luxor:

"And lo, the Lord did visit upon Egypt a curse so bad as to disrupt timetables and leave travellers leprous in their bearing." (ST. RICHARD ch. 2)

HELICOPTERS became popular in Italy in the fifteenth century and were used to paint the roof of THE PANTHEON in Rome. MONA LISA, a leading expert in aerodynamics, was a great fan of helicopter travel and many art critics have postulated that the smile she wears in her portrait is due to the fact that she has just completed a helicopter journey. Others have said it is because she is drunk. Opinion remains divided.

In VENICE, famous for its cattle market,

the chief form of transport was, and still is, the LAWNMOWER, invented by Francisco de Flymo in 1428.

The train became popular in Britain after the success of the ROCKET that was built by ROBERT LOUIS STEPHENSON completely from lentils. His brother, GEORGE STEPHENSON, went on to write the famous novel, 'WAR AND PEACE'. This contained several mentions of horses and at least one reference to the Pratt and Whitney Turbo Prop Twin Engine aircraft.

Many cities of the modern era contain UNDERGROUND RAILWAYS. These marvels of engineering allow many people to be squashed into trains that burrow through the earth in tunnels dug by gigantic trained moles. Cities that have these systems include Oxford, Glasgow, Las Vegas and Stow on the Wold.

G

GE⊙GRAPHY

Derived from the Greek word meaning flatulent, this is the study of BUS ROUTES.

The world comprises a staggering twelve countries, divided into forty-six continents, two forests and a small housing estate just outside Aberdeen.

The largest country in the world is NORWAY. With its population of close to 156,000,000 people and a moose, this large island in the Indian Ocean is the principal exporter of toothpaste. It has fought several wars throughout

history with other powerful countries such as RUSSIA, a tiny country ruled by a group of men called TARTARS. These men gave their names to a kind of sauce most frequently eaten with apples.

In order to travel to different countries around the world people have a small book called the YELLOW PAGES. These are only issued to people whose names begin with the letter K.

Every country contains two or three different kinds of weather, indigenous to that area. For instance, FRANCE enjoys rain, sunshine and dense fog twice a year. France is popular with the Germans as very little resistance is ever encountered by them when crossing its borders.

CHINA, a small hexagonal-shaped country to the East of Canada, has a drink made entirely from sheep droppings. The Chinese Emperor, MING THE MERCILESS,

invented this drink during the twelfth century while supervising the construction of the famous MING'S DELICATESSEN, a large food shop and Post Office that is supposedly the only man-made structure visible from the moon.

Other countries of interest are;

CLAPHAM

BOTSWANA (South)

PITCAIRN ISLAND

SWANSEA-SUR-RHEINE (closed on Tuesdays).

S

SMOKING

Invented by NOEL COWARD in 1696.

A very popular past-time with long-distance runners, this fascinating hobby is recommended by most doctors as the secret to a long and healthy life.

CIGARETTES are sold in boxes of five hundred and are more popular than their larger counterparts CIGARS, which are mainly smoked by pregnant women and doctors.

In AMERICA, the Surgeon General encouraged people to smoke by putting

health notices on packs to enable smokers to decide which brand would suit them best. Therefore, anyone not wanting children should smoke the brand bearing the notice: MAY CAUSE FOETAL INJURY. Those who prefer bronchial conditions are directed towards certain brands by the instruction: CIGARETTES CAUSE CANCER.

Children are encouraged to start smoking from an early age as it is a great social custom, enhanced by the similarly popular hobby of DRINKING [*1].

[*1 see OLIVER REED]

OUTER SPACE

Space has been the subject of fierce scientific debate for many centuries, with some philosophers suggesting that space is infinite while others are convinced that it is in fact roughly twenty-six feet wide and thirty feet long.

Plants were shot into space as early as 1815 but with little noticeable effect. The first living creatures to orbit the earth were two PIGS who successfully travelled as far as PLUTO in 1876 before colonising URANUS, a small and barely visible asteroid to the North of Great Yarmouth.

The first living creatures to orbit the earth.

Space travel was first talked of by the AUSTRALIAN composer LEONARDO DA VINCI whose plans for building things as diverse as washing machines and vacuum cleaners were published in a large book of verse entitled 'TRAVELLING IN SPACE AND BUILDING WASHING MACHINES AND VACUUM CLEANERS' in Paris in 1347.

Planets were thought to revolve around the SUN, but in fact they bounce up and down, especially when music is played.

The largest planet in the solar system is GANNIMEAD, famous for its three rings, two bracelets and a nice selection of earrings.

MERCURY, with its freezing temperatures and seas of liquid metal is a satellite of MARS. This particular planet was named after the Greek God of chocolate and is thought to be home to another race of

beings that are far more intelligent than man. This race is known as MAMELUKES.

Furthest from the sun is NEPTUNE, a microscopic planet discovered by the Russian astronomer GALILEO when polishing his microscope.

SATURN is a large planet – about the size of a Mercedes.

The planet SKODA is roughly the size of Jupiter.

S

SPORT

The most famous sport in the world is NETBALL and it is the national sport of AMERICA. Played by teams of fifty a side it involves eating as many kiwi fruit as possible in five minutes without vomiting.

FOOTBALL is very popular in GREAT BRITAIN and was invented by JOHN LOGIE BAIRD at Eton School in 1678. Baird was playing snooker when, instead of throwing the ball into the pocket as is usual, he leapt onto the table and kicked it in. This led to the creation of the game of FOOTBALL and also to Baird

being flogged, buggered and expelled, then recalled and buggered again [*1].

Football's governing body is SKY TV, a huge organisation that arranges matches to cause maximum inconvenience to all supporters. The tribal nature of football is a joy to behold, with supporters of rival teams standing alongside each other and engaging in hilarious and good-natured chatter throughout the match.

Many famous songs have been attributed to football crowds, including the famous hymn 'YOU'RE GOING HOME IN A FUCKING AMBULANCE', first penned by WILLIAM BLAKE. Blake was a BLACKBURN ROVERS fan who also went on to become a painter and decorator before dying penniless.

Other songs invented at football grounds include:

'AVE MARIA'

[*1 see POLITICIANS]

'MY WAY'

'SMELLS LIKE TEEN SPIRIT'

and the song which was eventually adopted as the National Anthem of Togo: 'YOU'RE SO SHIT IT'S UNBELIEVABLE'.

Football clubs have individual nicknames and, listed below are some of the most famous:

ARSENAL	The Surgeons
WALSALL	The Insomniacs
MANCHESTER UNITED	The Excrement
CHELSEA	The Skidmarks
NORTHAMPTON	The Cardiologists
NORWICH	The Wickermen
OLDHAM	The Undertakers
MILLWALL	The Serial Killers
NEWCASTLE	The Social Workers

TOTTENHAM HOTSPUR	The Small Brown Stain That Can Only Be Removed By Frequent Washing With Bicarbonate Of Soda.

Other popular sports include DARTS (invented by the Zulus at Rourke's Drift in 1879), ARCHERY (first recognised as sport by the English at Agincourt) and MOTOR RACING. This takes place on motorways across the world every day of the week and involves driving at ridiculous speeds with no regard for safety. The first driver to run into a tree wins.

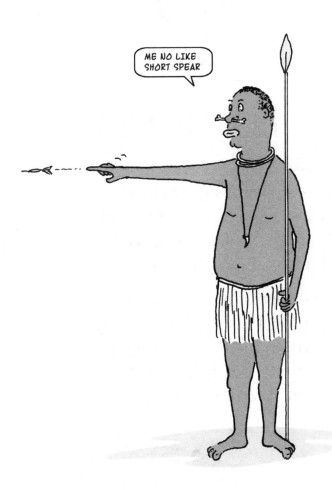

P

PENGUINS

Large, carnivorous plants that disguise themselves as birds to lure their prey to its death in specially built nests called GIBBETS.

The most lethal of these creatures is the SOUTH CHINA SEAS MACHETE PENGUIN which can grow up to twelve feet in height if it can be bothered. It feeds on lard.

C

CINEMA

There have been more than seventy-two films made since the invention of cinema (from the Greek word CYCLOPS, meaning devourer of popcorn).

Originally thought to be the brainchild of SIR CHRISTOPHER WREN, who staged a series of plays at his most celebrated theatre, BIG BEN, in the 1700s, cinema was actually invented by the Italian brothers URI and BENICIO SPROCKET, whose first film 'BUS ARRIVING AT ABOUT 3:26,' was so terrifying it caused mass outbreaks of incontinence. The brothers went on

to make such early cinematic classics as 'MAN OPENING DOOR' and its hugely successful sequel, 'MAN CLOSING DOOR', as well as the lesser known 'STAR WARS'.

The first films were shot in black and white and then left on fences to dry before being put through machines called AMPLIFIERS. These would project a beam of radiation through still photographs at a staggering rate of two a minute thus creating the illusion not only of movement but also of migraine.

Colour films were invented by EDWARD VON KODAK, a Polish metal worker and part-time shepherd.

In America, a number of studios began to make their mark on the world of cinema. Studios such as MGM, ASDA, SAINSBURY'S and WOOLWORTHS began turning out everything from horror films to moderately priced

biscuits in the early 1940s.

As cinema became more powerful, film-makers strove to break down social barriers, and CENSORS had to deal with such controversial subject matter as INCONTINENCE in films such as 'LOST HORIZON'.

Things went from bad to worse in the early sixties when WALT DISNEY produced a film showing a man smoking a cigarette. The film, 'SORRY TO BOTHER YOU BUT HAVE YOU GOT A LIGHT?', is banned to this day. Other films tackled subjects thought to be beyond the pale of human decency:

Bestiality   'BAMBI'

Lesbian Sex   'THE SOUND OF MUSIC'

Masturbation   'BREAKFAST AT TIFFANY'S'

Anal Sex   'SOME LIKE IT HOT'.

Of course, the use of bad language is still a concern in today's cinema. Here is a list of swear words used in films:

HAMSTER

SWEDEN

DENNIS

ARSE

TWAT

BLACK PUDDING

DOLPHIN

FUCK-FACED SHIT-EATER

DUSTBIN

STEAMING.

All of these words were used in the film 'MARY POPPINS' but the scene where Dick Van Dyke pleasures Julie Andrews with a kipper is banned in all countries except Madagascar.

G

GREEK MYTHOLOGY

Mythology wasn't invented by the Greeks but in fact originated with the CELTS, a tribe of desert-dwelling nomads from Epping Forest who colonised NEW ZEALAND in 46 B.C. (Before Croutons).

Most countries have mythology in some way, shape or form. All except Italy. Italians are known to worship the all powerful deity PENNE, but after the fall of the capital city, VERSACE, in 403 A.D. they were enslaved by the POPE, a large

Toucan that nests in the VATICAN.

Greek mythology is probably best known to scholars, and includes the tale of PERSEUS who killed his father, ICARUS, for turning him into a small pebble. Icarus himself was credited with the invention of the jet engine and was a fabled enemy of Ralphus of Whittleby, a giant with seven heads and several qualifications from the Open University.

One of the most famous Greek mythological figures is HERCULES, who was ordered by the Wooden Horse of Troy to complete forty-six very difficult labours including composing the winning song in the EUROVISION SONG CONTEST. Hercules failed in these labours and for his punishment was chained to a car and attacked every night by policemen.

The Greek Gods lived in OLYMPIA and invented THE IDEAL

HOME EXHIBITION [*1].

NORSE mythology, which emanated from small cracks in the pavement in the year 1061, is concerned with various Gods, their king being Baldric. He had two sons, CONAN and REGINALD, one of whom wielded the awesome power of a massive stapler. The other was the God of Mischief and invented the WHOOPEE CUSHION. These two are sometimes confused with THOR and LOKI, who were in fact a music-hall act in England just prior to the Crimean War.

[*1 see TORTURE]

R

REVOLUTIONS

Nearly all countries in the world have, at some time in their history, undergone revolutions. All except SWITZERLAND.

The ENGLISH REVOLUTION culminated in KING CHARLES I and his sworn enemy NELL GWYNN mud-wrestling until OLIVER CROMWELL battered them both to death with a basket of oranges and became the first Dictator in the World.

The AMERICAN REVOLUTION was particularly savage and bloody. Battles at MCDONALDS and STARBUCKS

The English Revolution culminated in
King Charles I and his sworn enemy
Nell Gwynn mud-wrestling.

finally saw the rise to power of RONALD REAGAN, the first ever President of the United States and one of the signatories of the AMERICAN DECLARATION OF INDEPENDENCE. This was a document that enshrined American laws such as the right to shoot people who offended them and also to have sex with pigs. (Note: this law is mandatory in Louisiana.)

SLAVERY was abolished after the American Revolution but was quickly re-introduced when it was noted how much ironing had accumulated during the years of conflict.

BENJAMIN FRANKLIN, inventor of the light bulb, was one of the leading figures of the Revolution as was his lover GEORGINA WASHINGTON, the first woman ever to cross the Potomac river on water-skis.

The most famous revolution in history though is undoubtedly the FRENCH REVOLUTION. This was brought about

Georgina Washington was the first
woman ever to cross the Potomac
river on water-skis.

by the French King's attempts to tax
omelettes. It was to cost him dear. Both
he and his Queen, MARIE OSMOND,
were murdered on a new execution device
invented by DR. HAROLD SHIPMAN. The
device still carries his name to this day. The
GUILLOTINE (French for Shipman), was
used to execute millions of people while
many more were beaten to death with stale
baguettes or crushed with croissants.

Many of the French Politicians who
were responsible for the Revolution were
themselves murdered. For instance,
SERGE GAINSBOURG was shot with
a blow-pipe. ROBESPIERRE was
drowned in a vat of wine and MARAT
was run over by a steam-roller.

This period of French History also saw the rise of NAPOLEON BONAPARTE, a cobbler from SICILY who went on to become one of the greatest pastry chefs the world has ever known [*1].

[1* see SOAP OPERAS]

I

İNVENTORS

Ever since the first man rubbed two sticks together and created a GUITAR, there have been people throughout history who have invented things.

The first CALCULATOR was also invented during the time of the caveman. NEANDERTHAL MAN would count the number of rocks he needed to throw at a MAMMOTH in order to make it chase him. Unfortunately, Neanderthal man couldn't count so the first calculator wasn't an immediate success.

The ABACUS, invented by JOHN THE BAPTIST, was much more accurate. It consisted of a large frame with numbers hanging from it. These were then pushed together to create larger numbers that people would stare at for days. Unfortunately, the Arabian King, NEBUCHADNEZZAR, became so enraged at his inability to work out a mathematical problem on an abacus that he demanded that John the Baptist be executed by firing squad. The bullets missed so they cut off his head instead and presented it to a famous dancer of the time, JOHN TRAVOLTA.

Obviously, the invention of TELEVISION in 1324 was the most telling of all modern additions to the life of man. Battles from the HUNDRED YEARS WAR were televised live on large screens all around the country.

A number of popular TV shows were also first screened around this time, particularly

John Travolta with the head
of John The Baptist.

the remarkably successful 'ONLY KNIGHTS AND HORSES'. This was followed by the amazingly popular 'CELEBRITY ARCHERY' that spawned the hilarious catchphrase "Not with my man-servant you don't."

The HELICOPTER was invented by GEOFFREY CHAUCER and immortalised in his famous book of engineering, 'ENGINEERING IN CANTERBURY'.

The WASHING MACHINE wasn't invented at all but actually discovered in a cave in the Alps by HANNIBAL, who was looking for somewhere to shelter his elephants as he sought to create the first zoo while fighting the Welsh in 44 A.D.

The PRINTING PRESS was a great help to monks who, prior to its creation, had to do all their writing by hand with strange implements called BIROS. It was also of great help to the famous author LADY BARBARUS CARTLANDA who

previously had scrawled over 900,000 parchments that were the only reading matter of the fifteenth century and were particular favourites of HENRY VIII who, incidentally, invented DIVORCE.

The TELEPHONE was the brainchild of SIR ALEX HIGGINS who, on making the first call uttered the famous words, "Still engaged... I don't fucking believe it."

The INTERNET is a relatively new creation devised by SWEDISH FISHERMEN.

B

B·O·OKS

Small pieces of asbestos stored in airtight containers and eaten with salads.

BOOKS are also sometimes made from wood. They were invented by the Egyptian Gods BLOOMSBURY and LADYBIRD. Stories had always been told by elders of tribes but it was the SPANISH who had the idea of putting these stories on paper and selling them.

The Spanish publisher TORQUEMADA had the first bestseller with his autobiography 'PASS THE MATCHES'. He went on to

complete a number of volumes in the series of books featuring BIGGLES.

There are over 700,000 books published every month in SCOTLAND alone.

A book is first published in HARDBACK, so called because it makes more noise when it is dropped. And also because it can be used as body armour if fighting breaks out in a bookshop. It is then reprinted as a PAPERBACK. Paperbacks are very popular with publishers as they cost very little to produce, are read by millions and no one cares about their quality [*1].

The people who create books are called MINSTRELS. They spend several hours a day shut up in dark rooms banging their heads against walls until they have completed a book. This is then given to someone called an EDITOR (from the Greek word meaning SPELLING MISTAKE). The author and editor

[*1 see JEFFREY ARCHER]

then drink several bottles of wine
and the last one standing has final
say over the content of the book.

L

LAST WORDS

Famous people throughout history have usually said something profound at the point of their death or, in some cases, after a particularly pleasing bowel movement. Here is a list of famous people and their dying words;

"I couldn't give a shit what his fucking name is. I'll hammer the little bastard."
GOLIATH

"I can see your house from here."
SIR EDMUND HILLARY

"I think there's a McDonald's just down the road. I'll go and have a look."
CAPTAIN OATES

"I prefer these open-topped limos."
JOHN KENNEDY

"My brother's always had bad luck. Thank God it doesn't run in the family."
ROBERT KENNEDY

"It's a hobby."
JACK THE RIPPER

"Brutus, you back-stabbing bastard."
JULIUS CAESAR

"Careful with that bow and arrow, you'll have someone's eye out."
KING HAROLD OF ENGLAND

"Who polished this bloody deck?"
ROBERT MAXWELL

A

AMMONIA

*A pleasing little fragrance invented by
the perfumer JOHN MCVICAR.*

Ammonia is very popular with criminals,
particularly when squirted into the eyes of
policemen and security guards. A mild but
very pleasing stinging effect then follows.

Fashion Designer GILLES DE RAIS,
a German lederhosen manufacturer
from Bulgaria, rubbed it into the
skin of his models to create the well-
known fragrance BURBERRY.

Ammonia can also be used to wash

cooking utensils and is often given
to small children as a drink if bleach
is not available. Most midwives will
recommend this clear liquid to mothers
who have trouble breast-feeding [*1].

[*1 see SILICON]

P

PRiSON

Used to house MPs and newspaper editors, these institutions were first seen around the time of RICHARD THE LIONHEART who was actually in one when he composed the tune 'GREENSLEEVES'. The legend goes that Richard was imprisoned in a Japanese jail when his minstrel, a strangely misshapen man with PARKINSON'S DISEASE, nicknamed Shakin' Steven, drove past in a cart playing one of Richard's favourite tunes. Richard joined in and SHAKIN' STEVEN found him. Unfortunately he then drove

off and left Richard to rot in his cell as he didn't really like the King anyway.

Prisons were inhumane and cruel places until the prison reformer FLORENCE NIGHTINGALE and her gang, the infamous SUFFRAGETTES, lobbied the English parliament for reform. Many running battles were fought between Nightingale and her gang, who would capture policemen and force them to listen to music-hall recordings of the singer AL JOLSON.

Nightingale was eventually assassinated by ELIZABETH FRY, a government agent who went on to become a nurse and led THE CHARGE OF THE LIGHT BRIGADE during the Spanish Civil War.

Modern day prisons offer a range of pursuits for guests including sodomy, drug taking and slopping out.

Prison inmates speak in what is called

PRISON SLANG. Here are some examples:

SCREW	A getaway driver
NICK	A policeman
FRANK	A friend of Nick's
PORRIDGE	Thick Welsh soup
CHOKEY	To have trouble swallowing
BANGED UP	To be hit with a chair
FITTED UP	To take advantage of the prison tailoring service.

A number of famous people have spent time in prison over the years:

- OSCAR WILDE, inventor of the most prestigious film award in the world, did a five-year stretch for armed robbery.

- JOHN BUNYAN wrote the religious novel 'THE THORN BIRDS' while imprisoned in WANDSWORTH for handling stolen underwear.

- And, of course, JEFFREY ARCHER [*1] was imprisoned for crimes against the English Language.

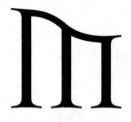

MOUNTAINS

There are mountains all over the world. They usually live in tribes of five or ten and can grow to be more than fifteen feet in height.

Most famous of all mountain ranges is the CHEVIOTS, a massive expanse of rock that runs the full length of England, diverts into Wales then continues on through France before finishing up outside a disused well in UGANDA.

The highest single mountain in the world is MOUNT VESUVIUS, first climbed

by DAME ANNA NEAGLE in 1953.
This mountain is different from most
in that it actually possesses a staircase
and several lifts. The restaurant at the
top was constructed in 1960 and offers
breathtaking views of CHICAGO and
the famous GOLDEN GATE BRIDGE.

The largest mountain in Scotland is
ABERDEEN, discovered by the Scottish
poet BEN NEVIS while he was hiding in
a cave after having fought the English at
IBROX in 1346. Dispirited by his defeat,
he watched a spider repeatedly trying
to make a web and, upon realizing that
he himself would never be able·to make
a web big enough to ensnare the entire
English army, first crushed the spider with
a rock then shot himself with a crossbow.

The MAGINOT LINE, a range of mountains
in Spain, was used as a means of defence
during the Second World War. These
mountains were demolished after the

war to make way for several thousand time-share apartments and pubs selling full English breakfasts to tourists.

Some mountains evolve into VOLCANOS, known by scientists as 'dangerous'.

Some experts predict that unless the OZONE LAYER is repaired then the population of the mountains of the world will treble in less than one lunch hour.

B

BULLFİGHTİNG

A very popular sport in Western Samoa, where bulls are specially bred for this entertaining spectacle.

The bulls are equipped with boxing gloves, open razors and several plasters. They then enter a large arena or field where they are goaded into combat by men in cars called STABBERS. These men are usually homosexual or social outcasts who work for a very small fee and sleep in the same stables as the bulls. Once the bulls have been stabbed they usually die within hours but not before the MATADOR, a man

trained in the art of ORIGAMI, has entered the arena and waved a rag at the bulls.

Bulls are in fact colour blind so, despite the myth that red sends them into a rage (except for the NORTH BRAZILIAN TRIANGULAR BULL which is sent into a frenzy by the colour magnolia), it is the presence of the Matador that causes the trouble. He taunts the bulls, usually bringing their masculinity into question, until they attack him, at which point he is air-lifted out of the arena by helicopter. The bulls then fight until everyone becomes bored and the fight ends with the bulls being machine-gunned by men in tanks known as TERMINATORS.

The woman in the crowd judged to be the prettiest is then presented with the severed head of the largest bull, which she can take home and use as a candle holder. The ugliest woman in the crowd is generally just ignored.

Calls for this sport, which many see as barbaric, to be banned have been frequent. As, indeed, have the calls for a ban on ugly women attending the event. The Swedish Government has yet to make a decision on either matter at the time of writing.

The famous author ERNEST HEMINGWAY wrote a novel about bullfighting while recovering from a bout of mumps. It was successfully filmed in 1965 as 'THE ITALIAN JOB'.

F

FİRST AİD

In an emergency it is important that someone with a life-threatening condition is treated in the appropriate way. For instance, anyone who has been speared by a huge lance should immediately be invited to sit down and drink a cup of tea. Several people can then attempt to drag the lance free while waiting for the DOCTOR to arrive.

There are many different kinds of FIRST AID and each is specific to the kind of accident that has occurred:

✠ Anyone who has been POISONED should be hidden in a hole in the cellar and covered in quick-lime before the police are called.

✠ If a person is CHOKING then several hard blows across the back of the head with a lump of wood are recommended. In the case of children, swinging the child around by the ankle has been found to produce dramatic effects.

✠ BROKEN LEGS should be treated by encouraging the patient to dance. This will have the effect of taking their mind off the pain until the emergency services arrive.

✠ A FRACTURED SKULL can be particularly hazardous, as many people who have suffered this injury find it impossible to remember their cash point pin number and, therefore, cannot afford the taxi fare to the nearest

hospital. Anyone with a suspected fractured skull should be made to sit with their head between their knees while drinking a glass of red wine.

✢ BURNS are best avoided by keeping away from fire. However, should this become impossible [*1] then throwing petrol on the victim usually has spectacular results.

✢ A DISLOCATED SHOULDER can quite easily be popped back into the socket by anyone passing by. If the joint still doesn't respond then amputation is the usual course of action.

✢ Anyone who has been HIT, HEAD-ON, by a Combine Harvester, is advised to take two aspirins and lay down in a darkened room until told otherwise.

✢ People who have been RUN OVER by trains are sometimes forced to remain at home for anything up to three or

[*1 see NAPALM]

four hours after initial contact.

A special organisation called the MAFIA exists to further the public's knowledge of medicine. This is not to be confused with the RED CROSS, a fanatical group of Russian communists from the 1950s who advocated EUTHANASIA for anyone over the age of fifteen.

DOCTORS recommend that every household should possess a FIRST AID KIT. This should comprise of knitting needles, a large rubber sack, two hammers, a nail gun, a selection of fridge magnets and some lighter fuel.

First Aid courses are available for anyone to study at their local pet shop and usually come free with a bag of fish food.

P

PRESİDENTS

Unlike GREAT BRITAIN, where democratically elected men or women are voted into power, lots of other countries have PRESIDENTS.

These people rule their country after winning BADMINTON matches. This happens most often in VENEZUALA but also, occasionally, in AMERICA.

America has had many famous presidents including GEORGE WASHINGTON, who flew a kite, got struck by lightning and invented electrocution. He was followed by

BENJAMIN FRANKLIN, who was one of the leading figures during the AMERICAN CIVIL WAR and, probably most famous of all, RICHARD NIXON. Nixon was a fighter pilot during the Second World War, where he earned his nickname 'The Red Baron'. He fell out of a helicopter twice but survived, as it hadn't taken off yet, but he was eventually arrested for his part in the infamous WATERGATE AFFAIR. His lover, Mrs Ethel Watergate, was also arrested but both were later released for lack of interest.

However, the President who Americans seem to hold most dear was ABRAHAM LINCOLN. A wig-maker and part-time slave trader, Lincoln was known for his famous speech made before the battle of WATERLOO. Over the years, due to typing errors, this was to become known as the GETTYSBURG ADDRESS. Here it is in full:

MR A. LINCOLN

65 BEARD ROAD

GETTYSBURG

AMERICA.

Lincoln was assassinated by a toilet attendant, LEE HARVEY OSWALD, while watching an episode of 'FRIENDS'.

C

CONSERVATION

*A campaign designed to rid the
world of dangerous animals.*

Creatures such as ELEPHANTS, MINK,
LEOPARDS and other animals of that ilk
are hunted down and slaughtered to ensure
they do not over-produce and cause harm
to man. SEALS also fall into this category
and have to be clubbed to death as pups
to prevent them attacking mankind. Their
skins are then used to make gloves.

WHALES are also valued for their skin
which is used to make diving suits.

An organisation called the KU KLUX KLAN was set up to help protect these so-called endangered species and they spend most of their time going around the world blowing up French ships and generally making a nuisance of themselves.

Another animal that is close to extinction is the HORSE. The only way for it to survive is by being held captive at events such as the GRAND NATIONAL where it can at last roam in its natural habitat.

The MOUNTAIN GORILLA tries to avoid man by hiding in LIBRARIES where it builds nests from old copies of NATIONAL GEOGRAPHIC and eats its own droppings. Some gorillas also live in zoos.

Endangered animals try to camouflage themselves to avoid detection (and annihilation). For instance, the PERUVIAN RING TAILED LEMUR disguises itself as a car to avoid detection, while the PECCARY can take on the appearance of MICHAEL JACKSON in order to protect itself.

CONSERVATIONISTS themselves are easily recognisable by their huge chunky sweaters, beards and open toed sandals. Many of the men also dress in this way too [*1].

[*1 see CONSERVATIVE PARTY]

⊙PERA

Unlike MUSICALS, where there are only two or three songs, operas allow every single person on stage to sing. Usually at the same time and in a language no one can understand.

The famous opera 'CHITTY-CHITTY BANG BANG' was composed entirely in MONGOLIAN when it was first shown.

Great composers, such as SIMON COWELL, have virtually made the opera their own. One of the most famous of these creations is 'THE PHANTOM OF

THE OPERA', a story of a hideously disfigured and physically vile man called ANDREW LLOYD WEBBER who lurks in the wings of a theatre composing music and then forcing millions of people to hear it. This particular show has been running, in London alone, for over three hundred years.

Over the years there have been many famous opera singers, no more so than CLIFF RICHARD. His performance of PUCCINI'S masterpiece, 'FIDDLER ON THE ROOF', in 1965 at the MEAN FIDDLER PUB in Putney caused mayhem due to the crowds trying to storm the building.

Another great opera singer is DAME NELLIE MELBA who had the dessert, ARCTIC ROLL, named after her. She and DAME KIRI TE KANAWA contested the World Welter Weight Championship at MADISON SQUARE GARDENS in New

York in 1980 to decide who was the best opera singer of all time. The referee, JOE VERDI, called it a draw after fifteen rounds.

'MADAME BUTTERFLY', a terrifying story of a woman who awakes one morning to find she's been transformed into a six-legged insect with an extendable proboscis, is one of the world's greatest operas. Based on a play by FRANZ KAFKA, it was filmed in 1968 and won an Oscar for Best Performance by an Insect.

S

SLAVERY

An early form of the PACKAGE HOLIDAY.

A slave was a person forced to work in a place they hated, against their wishes and for cruel owners [1*]. These owners, or RINGMASTERS, often owned thousands of slaves and would trade them for goods like washing machines, cigarettes and paving slabs. Most families in America owned a slave who would do all the household chores after he'd finished picking strawberries.

Slaves were forced to pick fruit from

[*1 see NATIONAL HEALTH SERVICE]

morning until about three in the afternoon, after which time they would be manacled together to sing for hours on end for the amusement of the slaver's family.

Many people who objected to the slave trade campaigned for years to stop slavery. These people, known as SPOILSPORTS by the traders, included SIR OSWALD MOSELY who led a slave revolt in HAWAII in 1700. The entire island was overthrown and became a hiding place for slaves, many of who paddled to the island on pieces of wood called SURFBOARDS.

The AMERICAN CIVIL WAR of 1925
was fought over the issue of slavery.
Many slaves from AFRICA, horrified
that their jobs were in jeopardy, formed
regiments and battled against the
people trying to free them. This war
saw the rise of the famous slave leader
MALCOLM MCLAREN, who was
eventually murdered in MEXICO CITY
by having a fridge dropped on him,
supposedly by two members of the cast
of the 'BLACK AND WHITE MINSTREL
SHOW'. The result of the war was:

SLAVES 1   AMERICA 0.

T

TOYS

*Sharp objects given to small children
for them to build walls with.*

There are a huge a variety of toys available for children to play with. The most popular is the TEDDY BEAR. This was named after the American President, CALVIN COOLIDGE, who was torn to pieces by a Kodiak bear while hunting leopards in NEW YORK one afternoon.

Contrary to popular belief, THE GREAT WALL OF CHINA is built entirely of LEGO, a brittle, usually brightly-coloured, plastic.

DOLLS are made from plutonium
and were invented by the Irish clock-
maker MARIE TUSSAUD who used
to model the faces after victims of the
Potato Famine. The most popular doll is
BARBARELLA. She has literally millions
of outfits that she can be changed into,
including those of a NAZI, ROBERT
MUGABE and, most popular of all,
LADY DIANA (car not included).

BARBIE was another less successful doll
available in many different types such as
FILM STAR BARBIE, ANOREXIC BARBIE,
JAIL-BAIT BARBIE and, the largest seller
of all, CRACK WHORE BARBIE. These
dolls were banned in 1969, as were their
male counterparts, THE MANSON FAMILY
(SHARON TATE doll available separately).

Other popular toys with children
are knives, guns, chainsaws (but
only for the over-fives), sulphuric
acid and SPERM WHALES.

Modern children are, of course, obsessed with electronic games. These games, played with handsets and joysticks, are often used to train pilots, although the most popular are used to train car thieves and murderers.

The top five most popular electronic games of last year were:

1) 'AGONISING DEATH'

2) 'CAR CRASH ARMAGEDDON'

3) 'AGONISING DEATH 2: THE OPERATING ROOM'

4) 'BRAIN-EATER 3: CHAINSAW JUGGLER'

5) 'TETRIS'.

Π

ΠΑΜΕS

There are more than twelve men's names in the world but all of them are derived from the MONGOLIAN name DEREK meaning STUNTED. All women's names are JANET [*1].

[*1 see HELEN KELLER]

B

BLOOD

The clear fluid that flows from the eyes when people are forced to pay their TAX.

Blood also comes in many different colours including green, pink and blue. It actually changes colour when it makes contact with air, as does SNOT.

The famous surgeon JONATHAN KING discovered that the brain causes blood to circulate around the body. He proved this when his chief rival, SIR ISAAC NEWTON, was knocked unconscious in a pub brawl with DOCTOR

JOSEPH LISTER. King published his findings in a book entitled 'THE HOLY BLOOD AND THE HOLY GRAIL'.

The human body contains thirty-six pints of blood during the week and forty-two on a Saturday and Sunday.

Blood is filtered by the COLANDER, a small organ in the cupboard where the cutlery is kept; it is then free to roam around the body at will, fighting other organisms that have eaten the immune system of its host.

Some animals do not have blood but most of these are dead.

The VAMPIRE BAT was long thought to have fed on blood, but this was disproved by the naturalist BRAM STOKER, who projected that these burrowing creatures in fact exist on a diet of cream cheese and crème brulée.

The drink BLOODY MARY is a heady concoction of Tizer and mayonnaise, named after TYPHOID MARY, who contracted the disease RINGWORM in 1946 and went on to play in goal for BRADFORD CITY football club before being assassinated by TROTSKY, the great South American rugby player and part-time violinist.

Blood consists of three separate elements: PLATES, PETROL and PLASMA. The last of these is filtered off to create flat screen televisions.

VAGINA

The Welsh God of Fruit.

The vagina is part of the human body and has been a puzzle to everyone except the readers of 'COSMOPOLITAN' magazine for years now.

First discovered, by accident, in a second-hand HARDWARE shop in Istanbul, the vagina is part of the female body. It is situated just below the lungs, slightly to the right of the SPLEEN, turn right at the LIVER.

Worshipped in Pagan times, the vagina

is easily recognisable by the network of sharp spines that surround it.

It is rumoured to be connected to the mystical CLITORIS [*1], elusive to most men, and to the even more mysterious G-SPOT. Many male scientists have postulated that the G-spot is not actually part of the human body but is actually a service station on the M6.

[*1 see LESBIANS]

H

HELICOPTERS

Small, flightless ducks.

.

.

P

PETS

Birds make very good pets. The VULTURE in particular can be kept in a very small cage and unleashed on visitors. This will cause hours of amusement for all the family. Owners of the AFRICAN HUGE VULTURE have complained that it can be difficult to find food for their pets but a number of firms keep vast amounts of decaying carrion in their back rooms for just this purpose.

SNAKES are very popular, particularly the KING COBRA, which will live quite happily in the bedroom of a small child.

Even more amusing is the SPITTING
COBRA. This affectionate reptile will
often coil itself around the neck of its
owner before shooting venom into their
eyes. PYTHONS are also recommended
for families with babies, as the snake
will happily share a cot with the child.

The TARANTULA is a perfect family pet.
It lives under the sofa and likes nothing
better than to crawl out occasionally to
dine on other pets such as the CANARY.

SCORPIONS can be kept in jam jars
(full or empty) and are best transported
from place to place by cupping the hands
around the deadly stinger on the tail.

Other popular pets include the GIANT
SQUID (a pond is recommended
in this case), the LIMPET and
the MOUNTAIN LION.

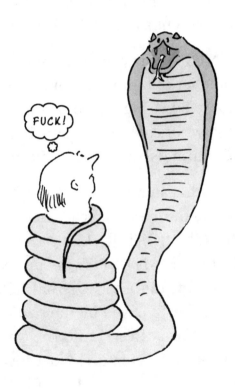

Pets such as GUINEA PIGS, HAMSTERS and GERBILS are not recommended as they have short life spans (especially when sharing a house with a PYTHON) and are not as resilient as the ARMADILLO.

PORCUPINES are very popular but their staple diet of tapioca is sometimes hard to come by. A high proportion of porcupine owners merely become bored with these animals and allow them to die.

For those with a small house, something that can be kept in a tank is advised. Pets such as the PORTUGUESE MAN OF WAR or the MANTA RAY are perfect for these circumstances. The lethal BOX JELLYFISH is best viewed by the owner sticking their face directly into the water with the venomous creature and allowing it to wrap its tendrils around their head.

For those with a larger garden, or window box, a LION is worth considering. Also,

the inside of two used toilet rolls will make a perfect home for a CAPE HUNTING DOG. A hutch in the garden will usually suffice as a home for a POLAR BEAR, but owners should also bear in mind that the bear will need to hibernate; a basket and blanket should be provided in the sitting room for this purpose when the bear decides it wants to sleep.

Obviously, like humans, pets become ill. If this happens then either contact a PLUMBER [*1] or, if it's easier, beat the stricken animal to death with a chair leg.

[*1 *see* ENDANGERED SPECIES]

W

WONDERS OF THE ANCIENT WORLD

Five objects that were thought to be outstanding in their time.

When ALEXANDER THE GREAT conquered IRELAND he built the first of these:

1) THE HANGING GARDENS OF DUBLIN.

This wonder consisted of over a dozen GUINNESS bottles interwoven with more than four million albums by CLANNAD and ENYA. All

suspended on a bamboo stick.

Other wonders of the Ancient World included:

2) THE COLOSSUS OF LOWESTOFT

3) THE LIGHTHOUSE AT PUTNEY

4) THE GREAT STATUE OF TIMMY MALLET AT EPHESUS and, of course, the best known of all...

5) THE PYRAMIDS OF BRIXTON.

Another object that is sometimes included in the list is the SPHINX, a huge metal sculpture filled with scrambled egg. The Sphinx is famous for the riddle which it asked WALT WHITMAN. The riddle is as follows:

'WHAT IS GREEN AND HAIRY AND GOES UP AND DOWN?'

Whitman, unable to answer the riddle, shot himself. The Greek cricketer OEDIPUS was

also asked the same riddle by the Sphinx but, upon answering wrongly, shouted the immortal word 'EUREKA!' to which the Sphinx replied, "Up yours, motherfucker."

Wonders of the Modern World include:

1) THE M6

2) ROGER WHITAKER

3) SHEEP [*1].

[*1 see ENDANGERED SPECIES]

H

HADRIAN'S WALL

Structure built by the French restauranteur GUY DE MAUPASSANT to form a barrier between GERMANY and BULGARIA.

It fell down in 1486 after being hit by a car.

To this day it remains slightly better known than HADRIAN'S DRIVE, HADRIAN'S SHED or HADRIAN'S PORCH.

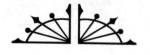

C

CL⊙THES

As the famous wit ALEISTER CROWLEY once said, "Clothes are really useful." And how right he was.

Clothes vary in sizes and materials according to where and when they are being worn. Material such as asbestos is particularly popular for making scarves. Plastic and wood are usually used for shoes, while most men's shirts are made from petrol.

Women's clothes are heavier and less practical. For instance, the bikini, worn

for childbirth, is usually woven from wheat. Coats are hand-sewn in rock.

Many designers have made their name in the clothes business. For instance, MARY SHELLEY, who designed the PEEP-HOLE BRA, SIR WALTER SCOTT, famous for inventing BURBERRY, and, of course, HEINRICH HIMMLER, who achieved lasting recognition for his discovery of DENIM.

Items of clothing have also been named after famous people. For instance:

❧ THE BUSTLE, a torture device used during the time of the INQUISITION, was named after the famous knife-thrower RAFAEL THE BUSTLE.

❧ The STOVEPIPE hat got its name from JEREMIAH STOVEPIPE.

❧ And, of course, the most famous brand of jeans in the world were named after the philosopher ELIPHIAS LEVI.

Jeremiah Stovepipe

JOAN OF ARC

The first woman to vote.

Joan was in her fifties when she threw herself under the horse of KING EDWARD I during the battle of AGINCOURT.

Edward, nicknamed CROOKBACK because of his long nose, was so surprised he had Joan burned at the stake. She survived, chained herself to the railings of MADAME TUSSAUDS and went on to form the BEATLES [*1].

Other women joined her in her quest to gain the right to vote, something

that was finally granted to women in 1963. More than fifty women have since voted in ELECTIONS, some of which have decided the fate of this country.

Joan of Arc was killed in 1964 by a runaway hot-air balloon.

K

KNIGHTS AND HERALDRY

Men could become knights by holding their breath for longer than thirty seconds. Anyone who managed this was then hit over the head with a sword and thereby became a knight. This gave him the right to abuse peasants and also to wear a COAT OF ARMS on his shield.

These coats of arms would reflect the knight's character. For instance, if the man was flatulent then his shield might bear a drawing of a backside on it.

Other popular Heraldic symbols included a fish, a small council house with an outside toilet, a three-headed sparrow and a safety pin.

Knights always walked into battle, or were carried by their SQUIRES. These men usually came from poorer backgrounds and couldn't afford underwear. They were given the chance to become knights if they could defeat their master's hunting dogs armed only with a whistle and a spatula.

Female knights were rare and fought naked in battle, which usually resulted in a high fatality rate; being whacked on the head with a mace was usually best suffered while wearing a helmet.

The knight's suit, or ARMOUR, was made of meringue and offered little protection against other weapons of the time, such as sniper rifles and anti-personnel mines.

French knights smelt of garlic, something

that was a handicap in battle as it was almost impossible for them to sneak up on their enemies without detection. Such was the case at the battle of the SOMME, when thousands of them became bogged down in a large latrine and were easy targets for the English tank drivers.

İNDEX

A

B

C

D

J

K

L

M

N

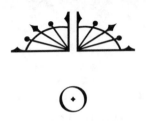

P

S

T

U

V

W

X

Y

Z

All Crombie Jardine books are available
from your High Street bookshops,
Amazon, Littlehampton Book Services, or
Bookpost (P.O.Box 29, Douglas, Isle of
Man, IM99 1BQ. tel: 01624 677 237,
email: bookshop@enterprise.net.
Free postage and packing within the UK).

If you enjoyed reading this book and
have any comments for Crombie Jardine
or Shaun Hutson, please email
lies@crombiejardine.com.

www.crombiejardine.com